Animals at Risk

Lydia Bailey

Illustrations by
Olena Kassian

SCHOLASTIC CANADA LTD.

Text copyright © 1993, 1999 by Lydia Bailey.
Illustrations copyright © 1993 by Olena Kassian.
All rights reserved.

No part of this publication may be reproduced or
transmitted in any form or by any means, electronic,
mechanical, recording or otherwise, or stored in an
information retrieval system, without the written permission
of the publisher, Scholastic Canada Ltd., 175 Hillmount
Road, Markham, Ontario, Canada L6C 1Z7.

For photocopying or other reprographic copying, a licence
must be obtained from CANCOPY (Canadian Copyright
Licensing Agency), 6 Adelaide Street East, Suite 900,
Toronto, Ontario M5C 1H6.

5 4 3 2 1   Printed and bound in Canada   0 1 2/0

Canadian Cataloguing in Publication Data

Bailey, Lydia
  Animals at risk

ISBN 0-590-51794-5

1. Endangered species — Juvenile literature. 2. Rare animals
— Juvenile literature. I. Kassian, Olena. II. Title.

QL83.B34 1999   591.68   C98-932876-7

Contents

Our world is full of wild animals. They live in the jungles and forests, in the mountains, in the water and in the wide open spaces. But many of those animals are in trouble. People have moved onto their lands and dumped poisons into their water. Hunters have killed too many of them. Some just don't have enough babies. As a result, many of them have become **endangered species**. That means it's possible that the whole group will die out and become **extinct**. They may disappear forever.

In this book you will read about a few of the animals at risk in our world. Some are big, some tiny. Some are playful, some shy. But each one is special and interesting. And they all deserve to live.

Do you wonder what it would be like to stay up all night? **Aye-ayes** don't have to wonder. They know. They spend most of the day asleep, curled up in little balls. But when the sun goes down, the aye-ayes wake up. Then they leap through the trees looking for insects and fruit.

Aye-ayes have very long fingers and toes. The middle finger is the longest of all. They use that finger for almost everything. They reach into tree holes and scoop out juicy insects for dinner. They also use it to scratch, comb their coats and clean inside their ears.

Aye-ayes feed mainly on insects and fruit. The few aye-ayes that are left are found in the rainforests of Madagascar, an island off the east coast of Africa.

What animal looks like a little dinosaur? The **giant armadillo** does. This animal may be timid and shy, but it doesn't have to be. An armadillo is protected by its own suit of armour. A coat of bony plates completely covers the top and sides of its body.

If an armadillo meets an enemy, it doesn't fight. Instead, it rolls up into a ball. At other times when it doesn't feel safe, it does just what you might do. It runs away as fast as its legs will carry it.

Some giant armadillos can still be found in South America, from Venezuela to northern Argentina.

If someone asked you how big a hippo is, you would probably say it's huge! So you might be surprised to learn that one kind of hippo is quite small. The **pygmy hippopotamus** is about the same size as a big pig.

Pygmy hippos live in the jungle. At night they walk slowly along paths they've made in the deepest part of the jungle. These paths are like tunnels through the thick leaves. They find fruit and tender green plants to eat as they go. Imagine having your supper in a leafy green tunnel!

The pygmy hippopotamus lives alone or in pairs in the lowland jungles of western Africa. It's often found along streams and in swamps.

Hisssssss! A mother **python** is sitting on her eggs. She coils her long body around nearly 100 eggs and rests her head on top. This is how she makes sure they stay warm and snug.

When it's time for a baby python to be born, it breaks a hole through its tough eggshell with a small, sharp tooth. Then out it slides and away it goes. Baby pythons don't need to stay with their mothers. They can take care of themselves from the minute they are born.

Full-grown pythons can measure over eight metres long. A few have been measured at more than nine metres!

Pythons are found in most tropical regions — western Africa, China, Australia and the Pacific Islands, central America, southern Asia, Indonesia and the Philippines.

13

Swoosh! Look up in the sky! Is that an airplane? No, it's a **California condor** soaring high among the clouds. The condor has very long black and white wings. It can glide through the air for long distances. It never even has to flap its wings.

The condor is beautiful when it's in the air. But not when it's on the ground. Then it's a lumpy, funny-looking bird. It has a hooked beak, small eyes and a wrinkly bald head. These can make it look quite mean. But don't be fooled. Condors are really rather timid and shy.

There aren't many California condors left. But you might be able to spot one in one of the protected areas near Los Angeles, California.

High on a mountain ridge in a misty forest lives the rare **golden toad.** How rare are these little toads? Very rare! They live only in one forest and nowhere else in the world.

When the spring rains come, golden toads play in the puddles. The male toads are a bright carrot-orange colour. They look like tiny jewels hopping about on the forest floor.

The last sighting of a golden toad was in Costa Rica in 1989. Scientists are investigating to see if the species is extinct.

What a strange-looking bird the **kakapo** is. It has a head like an owl and a body like a parrot. That's why some people call it the owl parrot.

The kakapo really is a parrot. It's the only parrot in the whole world that can't fly. These birds hop and run and climb to the tops of tall trees. And when they're ready to come down, they don't fly. They spread their wings and glide to the ground!

Kakapos used to be found everywhere in New Zealand. They are extinct now in most of the country, but they can still be found on nearby islands.

The **markhor** has snakes growing from the top of its head! Well, not really. But its long horns curl and look a lot like snakes. In fact, the word "markhor" means "snake horn."

These wild goats climb high up into the mountains. They jump easily from rock to rock. Markhors sometimes climb all the way out on a thin branch just to get to a tasty snack of leaves!

These animals can be tough too. One markhor will shake another right out of a tree so it can get the best leaves for itself.

Long ago markhors were plentiful in the Himalayan mountains of northern Pakistan. Now their numbers are greatly reduced.

21

Can you spot the **snow leopard** hiding in these rocks? Its thick grey-white fur makes it hard to see. And that suits the snow leopard just fine. These big cats are shy and like to live alone.

Snow leopards live high up in the mountains where it's cold and snowy. But the cold doesn't bother them. They have a beautiful fur coat to keep them warm. When they're sleeping, they wind their long tail around themselves like a scarf.

Snow leopards live in the mountains of central Asia. They can be found as far north as Russia and in countries all the way south to India.

Most wild yaks are found in the mountains of northern Tibet.

Imagine having hair so long that it almost touches the ground. **Wild yaks** need long, warm coats. They live on some of the tallest mountains in the world, where it's very cold. In their thick, shaggy fur coats, they can stand temperatures cold enough to freeze your toes. A baby yak stays nice and warm by snuggling up under its mother's cozy blanket of hair.

What swims like a fish, but has a name like a dog? Meet
Meet the **desert pupfish!** It's about the same size as a
small aquarium fish. And it's just as playful as a puppy.

The desert pupfish can stand water as cold as the
coldest swimming pool and as hot as the hottest bath.
Long ago, this tiny fish had large lakes and rivers to swim
in. But these dried up. So the pupfish were stranded in
small pools and springs in the middle of the desert. That's
why people call them a desert fish.

Some kinds of pupfish are already extinct. The
rest live in the southern United States and
northern Mexico. Scientists are trying to find
new homes for them before it's too late.

Have you ever heard of a cow that lives in the the water? That would be a **manatee**. Manatees are called sea cows. That's because they spend their days grazing on grass — sea grass, that is. Manatees have huge appetites. They spend seven or eight hours a day just eating.

A long time ago, sailors thought manatees might be mermaids. That's hard to believe. With their round bodies and curved flippers, they look more like small fat whales. But manatees aren't related to either whales or cows. Their closest cousin on land is the elephant!

There are three kinds of manatees: West Indian, Amazonian and West African. They are found in the areas they are named for.

You have to look fast and look hard if you want to see a **sea otter.** These little animals hardly ever stay still. They are always playing together — turning somersaults in the water, ducking each other or just paddling in the waves.

When sea otters are tired, they float lazily on their backs. They doze in the warm sun. At night they wrap themselves in a large seaweed called kelp so they won't drift away. Then they let the ocean waves rock them to sleep.

Not long ago, sea otters were almost extinct. Now scientists and other groups are trying to get their numbers back up. They are found along the north Pacific coast.

Can you imagine a bird that stands as tall as a 12-year-old child? Or one that likes to dance? That would be the **whooping crane.** The whooping crane makes a sad cry that sounds like a high-pitched horn. It has enormous white wings, fierce yellow eyes and a red-capped head. Some people say it's the most beautiful bird in North America.

The male whooper shows off to the female. He bows and flaps his fan-like wings. Then he jumps up and down. Soon the female joins him in a wild dance. The two birds continue to bounce up and down like jumping-jacks for a few minutes — or even hours.

Whooping cranes spend their winters along the gulf coast of Texas. They spend the rest of the time in the Northwest Territories and Alberta. That means they travel almost 4000 km twice each year!

Most black-footed ferrets are found in the state of Wyoming in the United States. Some are coming back to Montana and South Dakota as well.

There's a masked bandit loose on the plains tonight. It's the **black-footed ferret.** This small sausage-shaped animal has a mask of black fur across its face. Like most thieves, the ferret prefers to work at night so it can't be seen. What's it looking for? Probably its favourite dinner — a prairie dog.

When the sun sets, the ferret slips quietly down into a prairie dog burrow. It creeps through the long tunnel, looking for a sleeping prairie dog. Then . . . *pounce!* The black-footed ferret has its dinner.

Did you know that dragons aren't just found in fairy tales? There really are dragons alive today. The **Komodo dragon** is a giant lizard with a long yellow tongue and a strong tail. Its teeth are as sharp as daggers. And its claws can rip apart a goat, a pig or even a grown-up person!

Komodo dragons are big and fierce after they grow up. But when they are young, they are tiny. They live high up in trees and they don't like to come down to the ground at all. Why? If they did, a bigger Komodo dragon might attack them!

If you want to see a wild Komodo dragon, you'll have to visit one of the islands east of Bali in the South Pacific Ocean.

The **puna rhea** looks like a small, skinny ostrich. And like ostriches, rheas can't fly. But they can run as fast as a galloping horse. Puna rheas live on cloud-covered plains high up in the mountains. They run across the plains with one long wing stretched out to the side, like the wing of an airplane.

A male rhea cares for the eggs of a number of different females. First, he scrapes out a nest. Then the females line up around it to lay their eggs. The male sometimes helps by using his wing to roll an egg into the nest. Then he sits on the eggs. And when the babies hatch, he looks after them all by himself.

The word "puna" means "high plateau." You can find rheas on the grassy plains of the Andes mountains in South America.

39

What creature creeps and crawls and is even older than some dinosaurs? The tarantula, that's what.

The **red-kneed tarantula** gets its name from the red hairs that grow all over its legs. This spider is so large that it can't spin a web strong enough to hold itself. Instead, it lives in a burrow under the ground. A female tarantula spends hours and hours spinning a silken sack for her eggs. After the tiny spiders hatch, they help their mother spin a nursery web. They live in this until they are ready to go off on their own.

Tarantulas can live a long time. One was known to have lived for 30 years!

Red-kneed tarantulas make their homes in Mexico.

EXTINCT

The **Barbary lion** used to live in the mountains of North Africa. It had a long, flowing golden mane and truly looked like a king of the beasts. But hunters killed too many of them. And too many people came to live on their lands. Now there's not a single one left. The last Barbary lion was killed in 1922.

EXTINCT

At one time, thousands of **Carolina parakeets** lived in the eastern United States. They lived in the forests of North and South Carolina, Virginia and Louisiana. They were hunted for sport, food and for their colourful feathers. Now there are none left. This small, playful green and yellow parrot became extinct in 1914.

EXTINCT

Once hundreds of thousands of **great auks** lived on rocky islands in the North Atlantic Ocean. They made their homes off Newfoundland, Nova Scotia and Iceland. Some even came into the Gulf of St. Lawrence. A few were found as far south as Florida, Spain and Italy. People killed them for food and for their attractive black and white feathers. These birds became extinct in 1844.

EXTINCT

The **quagga** looked like a mixture of half horse and half zebra. Not so long ago, great herds of these wild horses galloped across the plains of Africa. But people killed them for their meat and their beautiful striped skins. Now the quagga has disappeared from the earth forever.

Where Are They?

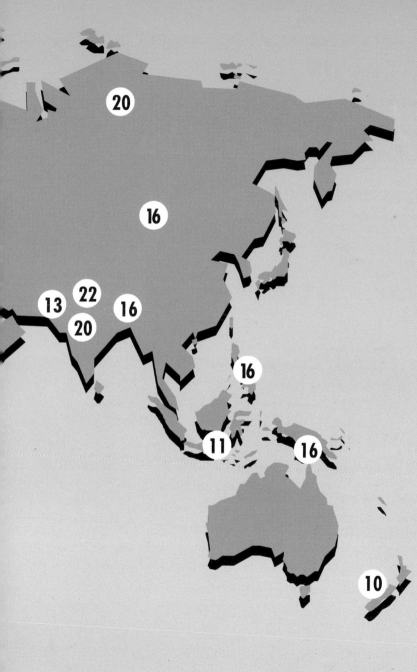

1. aye-aye
2. Barbary lion
3. black-footed ferret
4. California condor
5. Carolina parakeet
6. desert pupfish
7. giant armadillo
8. golden toad
9. great auk
10. kakapo
11. Komodo dragon
12. manatee
13. markhor
14. puna rhea
15. pygmy hippopotamus
16. python
17. quagga
18. red-kneed tarantula
19. sea otter
20. snow leopard
21. whooping crane
22. wild yak

Other Endangered Animals

Here is a list of some more animals at risk. It may surprise you to see some of these animals on an endangered list. But it's true. Even some very familiar animals are dying out as fewer and fewer of them survive in the wild.

American Crocodile

Bactrian Camel

Blue Whale

Cheetah

Chinchilla

Elephant

Giant Panda

Green Turtle

Grizzly Bear

Hairy-Nosed Wombat

Humpback Whale

Lion

Mediterranean Monk Seal

Mountain Gorilla

Mountain Lion

Orangutan

Polar Bear

Queen Alexandra's Birdwing Butterfly

Red Wolf

Rhinoceros

Spotted Owl

Tiger